ROSEN ✔ *Verified*
CURRENT ISSUES

HOMELESSNESS

Xina M. Uhl

ROSEN
PUBLISHING
New York

Published in 2021 by The Rosen Publishing Group, Inc.
29 East 21st Street, New York, NY 10010

First Edition

Editor: Amanda Vink
Book Design: Reann Nye

Photo Credits: Cover ljubaphoto/E+/Getty Images; Series Art PinkPueblo/Shutterstock.com; p. 5 FREDERIC J. BROWN/AFP/Getty Images; p. 7 Maps Expert/Shutterstock.com; p. 9 PhotosbyAndy/Shutterstock.com; p. 10 Agence France Presse/AFP/Getty Images; p. 11 (top) Robert Alexander/ Archive Photos/ Getty Images; p. 11 (bottom) Bettmann/Getty Images; p. 12 SpeedKingz/Shutterstock.com; p. 13 Patricia Spencer / EyeEm/Getty Images; pp. 14–15 Bloomberg/Getty Images; p. 17 Andrew V Marcus/ Shutterstock.com; p. 19 Frederic Legrand - COMEO/Shutterstock.com; pp. 20–21 Matt Champlin/ Moment/Getty Images; pp. 22, 23 NurPhoto/Getty Images; pp. 24–25 https://commons.wikimedia. org/wiki/File:Alaskan_Viaduct_Homeless.jpg; pp. 27, 37 The Washington Post/Getty Images; p. 29 Jeff Greenberg/Universal Images Group/Getty Images; p. 30 MediaNews Group/Bay Area News via Getty Images/MediaNews Group/Getty Images; p. 31 Supawadee56/Shutterstock.com; p. 33 Pekic/ E+/Getty Images; p. 34 Jonathan Weiss/Shutterstock.com; pp. 38, 39 Andy Cross/Denver Post/Getty Images; p. 41 Portland Press Herald/Getty Images; p. 43 Greg Doherty/Getty Images Entertainment/Getty Images; p. 45 SDI Productions/E+/Getty Images.

Library of Congress Cataloging-in-Publication Data

Names: Uhl, Xina M., author.
Title: Homelessness / Xina M. Uhl.
Description: New York : Rosen Publishing, [2021] | Series: Rosen verified: current issues | Includes index.
Identifiers: LCCN 2020005114 | ISBN 9781499468434 (Paperback) | ISBN 9781499468441 (Library Binding)
Subjects: LCSH: Homelessness–United States. | Homeless persons–United States. | Homelessness–United States–Prevention.
Classification: LCC HV4505 .U35 2021 | DDC 362.5/920973–dc23
LC record available at https://lccn.loc.gov/2020005114

Manufactured in the United States of America

Some of the images in this book illustrate individuals who are models. The depictions do not imply actual situations or events.

CPSIA Compliance Information: Batch #BSR20. For Further Information contact Rosen Publishing, New York, New York at 1-800-237-9932.

Find us on

CONTENTS

HOW DOES IT HAPPEN?

More than half a million people in the United States are homeless on any given night. Some people live in temporary, or limited time, housing. These places may be public or private **shelters**. Other people sleep in open areas or empty buildings. These are places not meant to be lived in.

Someone can become homeless for many reasons. They might suffer from a costly health problem. They might have a mental illness or issues with drugs and alcohol. Maybe they don't have a job, and they can't afford to pay for a home. Sometimes they don't have friends or family to help them.

No person shall sit, lie or sleep in or upon any street, sidewalk, or other public way.

Some people don't like seeing camping tents on city streets. But for the people living in them, they are a way to get shelter from the weather.

HOMELESSNESS LOOKS LIKE...

Some people who are homeless are single. Other times, an entire family is homeless. A person who has been sleeping outside may look dirty. But someone who is homeless and sleeping in their car may look like a business **professional** during the day.

It's often hard to tell if a person is homeless. They may look just like everyone else. Sometimes people are homeless for a long time. Other times, it's just for a few days or weeks.

DEFINING HOMELESSNESS

These are the four categories of homelessness:

1. Having no regular, stable place to live

2. Being about to lose your home

3. Being under 25 and without a regular home for the past two months

4. Trying to get out of a violent home and having no other place to live

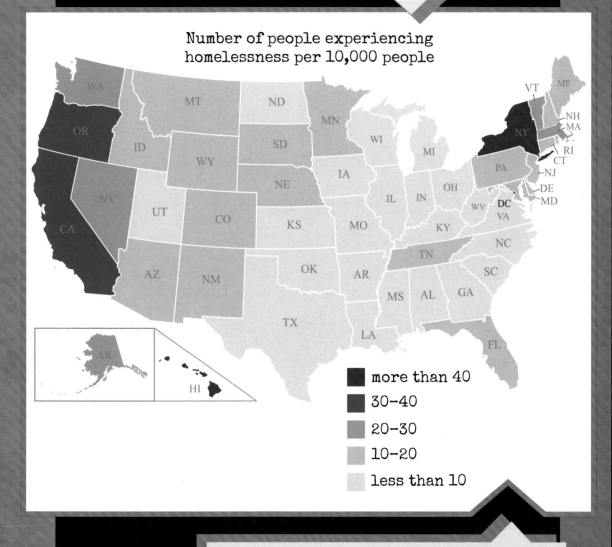

Number of people experiencing
homelessness per 10,000 people

- more than 40
- 30-40
- 20-30
- 10-20
- less than 10

This map shows the rough number of homeless people
in each state as of January 2018. The largest numbers
are in the District of Columbia, New York, Hawaii,
Oregon, and California.

WHAT DRIVES HOMELESSNESS?

Poverty lies at the root of most homelessness. People who don't make enough money often have to choose what bills they pay. Sometimes they go without food, or they go without heat in the winter. Other times they can't pay for housing.

When a person doesn't pay rent, they risk being evicted. That means they're kicked out. The bank also may **foreclose** on a person's house if they don't pay their **mortgage**. The person may become homeless if they can't find other housing.

✅ **VERIFIED**
To find out more about the causes of homelessness, see:
https://nationalhomeless.org/ about-homelessness/

Evictions are handled by the courts. Here, the police post a notice. The notice says that whoever lives there must leave.

HISTORY OF HOMELESSNESS

Homelessness in the United States isn't new. In the days of European **expansion** and creation of **colonies**, there was fighting. This was between European settlers and Native Americans. It forced many from their homes. In 1730, the first almshouse opened in New York. This was a place where homeless people, people with mental illness, and others could go for work and a place to stay. Still, there were problems. These places often weren't very clean.

WESTWARD EXPANSION

Homelessness became a national issue after the Civil War. More people moved to **industrialized** cities. The railroad also allowed people to move westward. Some looked for gold. Some people were looking for work. However, there weren't enough jobs to go around.

Today, **veterans** make up 7 percent of the homeless population. That amount has been dropping since 2011.

When the stock market crashed in 1929, many people lost their savings. Unemployment went up. Homeless people built shantytowns, which they named "Hoovervilles" because they blamed President Herbert Hoover for his inaction.

THE BIG HOUSE

Men make up 70 percent of the homeless. Minorities are more at risk. Young people under age 25 make up 7 percent of the homeless. Many of them leave difficult living situations at home. They may be **LGBTQ**. Many of these young people run away from home. Others are kicked out by their families.

Many young people become homeless after leaving child welfare programs such as foster care. LGBTQ youth, youth of color, and young people with children are more at risk.

Every year, 600,000 people get out of prison. There are a total of 5 million ex-cons living in the United States.

People freed from prison are at a great risk of becoming homeless. Housing and work are hard to find. A lot of landlords don't want **ex-cons**, or people who were formerly in jail, living in their property. Many managers don't want to hire them.

PRICED OUT

The number of homeless Americans went down between 2007 and 2018. However, it rose again in 2019. Homeless populations went up by 16.4 percent in California. Government officials from President Donald Trump's administration went to California in September 2019 to learn more. One major reason was high rents.

High housing costs have driven people to live in their RVs, even when they have jobs. These RVs are in the Bay Area. They're parked on a neighborhood street.

HOMELESSNESS IN BIG CITIES

In Los Angeles, many homeless people live in Skid Row, an area downtown. People live on the sidewalks. This causes unhealthy conditions. Trash and human waste are all around. Illnesses spread easily. Shoppers avoid nearby businesses. Homeowners don't like to look at the mess.

Homeless people may bother others on the street. They **panhandle** for money. Sometimes those with mental illness yell at things that aren't there. Drug addicts take drugs in plain view.

PROBLEMS WITH SHELTERS

There are some homeless shelters in cities like Los Angeles. Here, people can have a bed for the night. They might get meals. But they can be unsafe places. They also have rules that some homeless people dislike.

The mild weather in Los Angeles allows homeless people to camp out in public places.

MAKING THE HOMELESS CRIMINALS

The homeless are often seen as a problem. They panhandle for money, and business owners don't like them **harassing** their customers. Homeless camps can be dirty and often spread diseases.

Sometimes, citizens ask their city government to take action. One action may be sweeps. This is when the government bulldozes homeless camps. Some people believe sweeps are not only unhelpful but also very harmful to homeless populations.

AN IMPORTANT RULING IN 2019

Homeless people in Boise, Idaho, took the city to court. The city was putting them in jail for sleeping outside. The court ruled in their favor. Now it's against the law for the city to jail people when they have nowhere else to go. Cities across the country have started to follow this ruling.

Here, city workers clean up a homeless camp. They take tents, trash, and belongings to the dump.

FAST FACT
SOME PEOPLE THINK SWEEPS ARE NEEDED TO KEEP STREETS CLEAN. SOME SWEEPS ARE DONE WITH NOTICE OF AT LEAST 24 HOURS. OTHERS ARE NOT.

THE COUNTRYSIDE

Small towns and **rural** areas have homeless people too. It's harder to count the numbers. There aren't as many homeless shelters. But studies show that poverty is actually greater outside of cities.

Small towns often have few places to work. They can be far away from hospitals, grocery stores, and schools.

THE EMPLOYED HOMELESS

"Get a job!" some people tell the homeless. Yet, in any given month, about half the members of the homeless population are working. They just don't make enough money to cover all their expenses.

Some costs, such as childcare, are high. Vehicles to get to work are costly. They require gas, **insurance**, and repairs. Some areas have public transportation such as buses and trains, but they may not run regularly enough. It can take hours to get places.

Workampers may pack boxes like these. Amazon isn't the only place for seasonal work.

WORKAMPERS

Amazon hires hundreds of people for seasonal jobs. These only take place during certain times of the year. One group of seasonal workers is called workampers. They live in RVs at free campsites. They do hard work during shifts that last 10 hours or longer. Some walk more than 15 miles on hard concrete floors in large warehouses. People who are employed as workampers are often a step away from being homeless.

A DANGEROUS LIFE

The homeless face many dangers in their lives. In addition to illness, they can face **violence**. People sometimes throw things at the homeless. People steal their belongings. Sometimes the homeless are attacked. Women may fear rape, or unwanted sexual relations.

Weather is another danger. Heat waves harm those who live outside. Cold winters can also be very dangerous to them. Some find shelter in subways or other public places. Homeless shelters can fill up quickly.

There is often a lack of mental health doctors in rural areas. This means many homeless with mental health issues go untreated.

RURAL HOMELESS

Homeless in rural areas are more likely to be:

- Female
- Married
- White
- Currently employed

This homeless camp is in Seattle. People living outside here face many health challenges.

A DIFFICULT ISSUE

Fixing homelessness isn't as simple as just giving people a place to live. Most people need more help. Here are the ways that homelessness could be helped:

- **Job training.** This helps people learn skills. People with more skills typically earn better salaries.

- **Affordable housing.** This includes homes and apartments that cost less than other housing in the area.

- **Health care.** The costs of health care drive some into homelessness. Lowering the costs would help many people.

- **Mental health care.** Often, people with mental health problems don't get treatment. This can lead to homelessness.

- **Substance abuse treatment.** Drug and alcohol problems make it hard for people to keep jobs. These people are often sent to jail.

- **Food.** Food is a necessary expense. Without food, people can't live.

- **Care for children.** Parents need childcare in order to work and go to school.

The problems that cause homelessness can be costly to fix. Many people are working on these issues.

TAKING ACTION

The United States Interagency Council on Homelessness (USICH) was created in 1987. Its job is to organize the response of the **federal** government to homelessness. The policy was to provide housing to homeless people first. Then they could make other improvements in their lives. The program was successful overall. Since 2010, chronic homelessness has decreased by 22 percent. In 2017, Congress made the decision to keep the agency. In January 2020, President Trump appointed Robert Marbut as executive director. Some people worry about this change. Marbut has a record of pushing for heavy policing of homeless populations.

HELPING THE HOMELESS

Baylor University did a study in 2017. It showed faith groups did a lot to help the homeless. Catholic Charities runs many programs in the United States for the homeless. They gave nearly 1 million people beds for at least a night in 2018. Jewish Family Services helps many homeless people too.

The Salvation Army is another Christian charity. They provide shelter, food, and addiction services.

THE PRIVATE WORLD

Companies and individuals may donate, or give, to the homeless. Many people give money, clothing, and other goods to charities. Charities may be **nonprofits**. They don't pay many taxes. Volunteers give their time to serve food at soup kitchens. They collect things such as clothing, shampoo, and soap. They do other things to help raise money.

Disasters such as earthquakes and floods destroy homes. This causes widespread lack of housing. The American Red Cross helps people in disaster zones in the United States.

Apple makes phones, computers, smartwatches, and more. It's one of the richest companies in the United States.

BIG TECH

In 2019, Apple gave $2.5 billion to fight high housing costs in California. Facebook gave $1 billion for a similar program. Microsoft gave $500 million to help the Seattle area.

Google, Apple, and Facebook have also been **criticized**. Some people say that they've driven up costs. Their employees all need homes. This causes prices to rise for the available units in their areas. Some people believe big donations aren't enough to help the problems enough.

THE GOVERNMENT

The biggest provider of help is the government. This includes federal, state, and local governments.

FEDERAL HELP

The federal government covers the whole country. The 19 agencies that work with USICH on homelessness include the United States Postal Service (USPS) and Veterans Affairs (VA). The Department of Housing and Urban Development (HUD) and the United States Department of Health and Human Services (HHS) are a big part of this effort. These agencies study the problems. They also give out grants. Grant money goes to organizations all over the country. One of the actions has been to help veterans. Since 2011, the number of homeless veterans has dropped by 43 percent. Some people in government want to end homelessness across the United States.

Veterans have done a lot for their country. War leaves scars on bodies and minds. Because of that, they are at risk.

TYPES OF WELFARE

The federal government also gives money directly to people. This is called welfare. There are different kinds. Homeless people may or may not receive help of these kinds. Each state may have different requirements.

WE
Accept

SNAP
Supplemental
Nutrition
Assistance
Program

Welfare programs are often called entitlements. Congress often fights about the budget for these items.

SUPPLEMENTAL SECURITY INCOME
(SSI)

The Social Security Administration (SSA) runs this program. It provides cash assistance to certain U.S. residents who make below a certain amount, who are 65 or older, or who are blind or disabled.

SUPPLEMENTAL NUTRITION ASSISTANCE PROGRAM
(SNAP)

Each state runs this federal program. It provides benefits to low-income people in the form of a transfer card, much like a debit card. The money can be used to buy food.

CHILDREN'S HEALTH INSURANCE PROGRAM
(CHIP)

This program is a partnership between federal and state governments. It provides low-cost health coverage to children.

TEMPORARY ASSISTANCE FOR NEEDY FAMILIES
(TANF)

The federal government gives grants to states in order to run this program. It provides limited assistance to families with children.

MEDICAID

This is federally funded health insurance for the poor. Each state may call this program by a different name.

STATE AND LOCAL ACTIONS

The federal government gives grants to agencies, or organizations created for a purpose. These agencies can belong to states. They can belong to cities or counties. Grants can also go to private or religious charities to help with their services.

One federal program is called Health Care for the Homeless (HCH). It works to provide primary health care to the homeless. In 2017, 299 health centers got funding through this program.

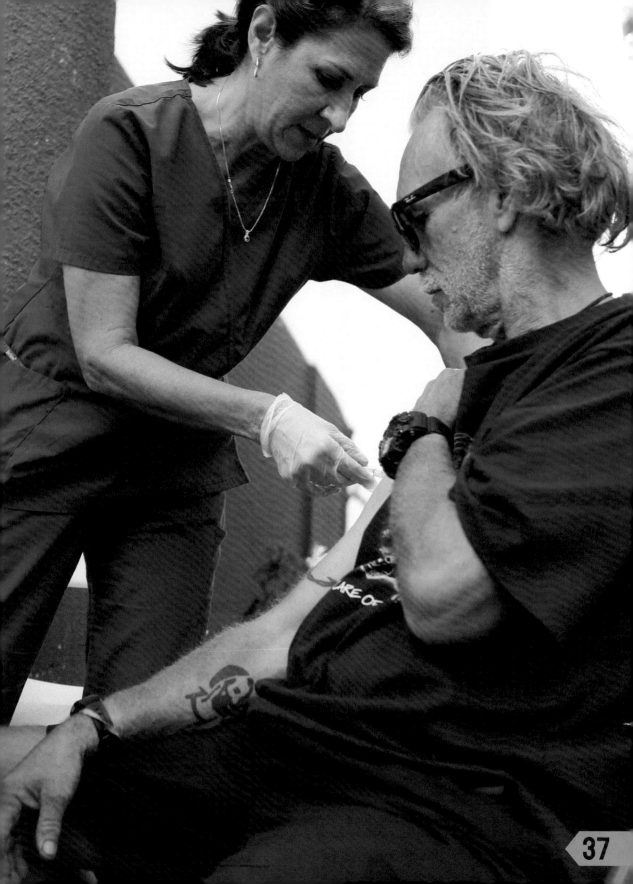

LOCAL SPENDING

States and cities don't just use federal money. They get money from taxes to spend locally. For example, many homeless people need job training. They may be working at unskilled jobs. They make little money. They may need schooling to get better-paying jobs. Classes may help them to write better and do math better. A local college may receive money to offer these services to the homeless.

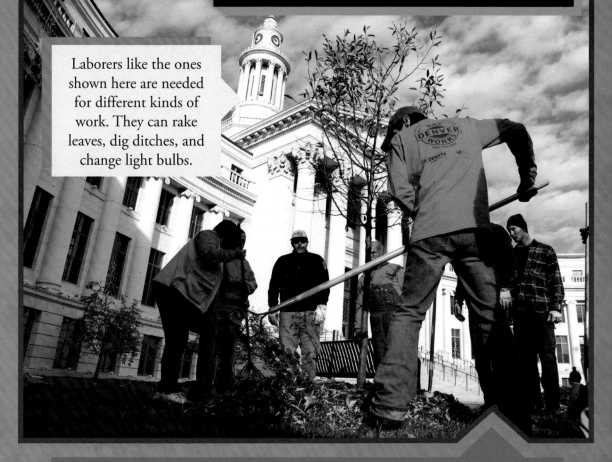

VERIFIED

More information on Denver Day Works can be found at this website:
https://www.denvergov.org/content/denvergov/en/denver-human-services/be-supported/jobs/denver-day-works.html

Laborers like the ones shown here are needed for different kinds of work. They can rake leaves, dig ditches, and change light bulbs.

DENVER DAY WORKS

The city of Denver, Colorado, has a program called Denver Day Works. The program hires people one day a week for 10 weeks. Each workday, workers receive breakfast, lunch, and a bus ticket. They are paid $70 cash per day.

NEW APPROACH

Portland, Oregon, has started a two-person Street Response team. These employees are crisis workers, not police officers. They will help the homeless, not take them to jail.

Austin, Texas, has a similar team. They assist the police on patrols. As of 2020, the city of Austin has opened 50 new housing units for those who've been homeless. The city is also building a new shelter.

FAST FACT

MANY HOMELESS PEOPLE HAVE ADDICTIONS TO OPIOIDS, A KIND OF DRUG. THE 2020 FEDERAL BUDGET SETS ASIDE NEARLY $5 BILLION FOR ADDICTION TREATMENT.

Often, crisis workers can connect those experiencing homelessness to programs that can help. This can be in the form of temporary housing or permanent housing.

HOW YOU CAN HELP

The homeless face big problems. Many people work to help solve them. Some people help at soup kitchens. Others join group efforts.

Even young people can help. Tyler Stalling is only eight years old. He heard that some veterans are homeless. He came up with the idea for Hero Bags. These bags have food, bedding, clothes, and bath products. He gives them to homeless vets.

The USPS runs a food drive every year called Stamp Out Hunger. People put food by their mailboxes to be picked up.

MORE TO BE DONE

Between 2007 and 2018, the number of homeless Americans went down. However, it rose again in 2019. Many more homeless were reported in California. The rate was up 16.4 percent. Government officials went to California in September 2019 for more information. They said thousands became homeless because of the economy, mental illness, the criminal justice system, and the housing market.

Most homeless people don't stay that way. Only about 25 percent are chronically homeless. Helping homeless populations takes time, hard work, and the right policies. But it's a problem we can solve.

✔ VERIFIED

There are many ways to volunteer. One organization is called Habitat for Humanity. Here's its website: **https://www.habitat.org/volunteer.**

Despite the many challenges, there is reason to hope.
You can do your part by volunteering!

GLOSSARY

colony: An area controlled by another country that's usually far from it.

criticize: To find fault with something or someone.

ex-con: A person who has been to prison.

expansion: The act of making something bigger.

federal: Relating to the central government of the United States.

foreclose: A legal action in which a bank takes possession of a home.

harass: To create a hostile or unpleasant situation for someone through unwanted contact.

industrialize: To develop industries and factories.

insurance: A thing that provides protection against a possible problem.

LGBTQ: Lesbian, gay, bisexual, transgender, and queer/questioning.

mortgage: A loan from a bank that a person takes out in order to buy a house.

nonprofit: An organization that doesn't pay most taxes, usually created for the public good.

panhandle: To beg for money on the street.

poverty: The state of being poor.

professional: Someone who does a job for a living.

rural: Relating to living in the country.

shelter: A place that offers protection.

veteran: A person who has served in the military.

violence: The use of bodily force to hurt, harm, or destroy.

INDEX